MW01600758

THE COMPLETE IPAD 8TH GENERATION USER GUIDE

The Illustrated Step By Step Manual with Tips to Master the New iPad

By

Connor Albright

The Complete iPad 8th Generation
User Guide

TABLE OF CONTENTS

CHAPTER ONE

How to multitask on your iPad

Your Apple iPad is capable of multitasking by offering two different multitasking modes: Slide Over and Split View. Slide Over allows you to view two apps on the screen with one app opening in a narrow pane which floats on top of the other while Split View allows you to open two different apps or allows you to open two windows from the same app which is done through splitting the screen into views that are resizable. You can, for example, open Maps and messages at the same time in Split View or open two message windows in Split View and also manage two conversations at the same time.

To open a second item in Split View, follow the steps below:

1. To reveal the Dock, swipe up from the bottom edge and pause. This should be done while you are making use of an app.

2. Press and hold an app in the Dock, then drag it to the left or right edge of the screen, and then lift your finger.

3. If both times are already in Split View, you can drag over any item that you wish to replace.

4. Drag the divider to the center of the screen to give equal space to both views.

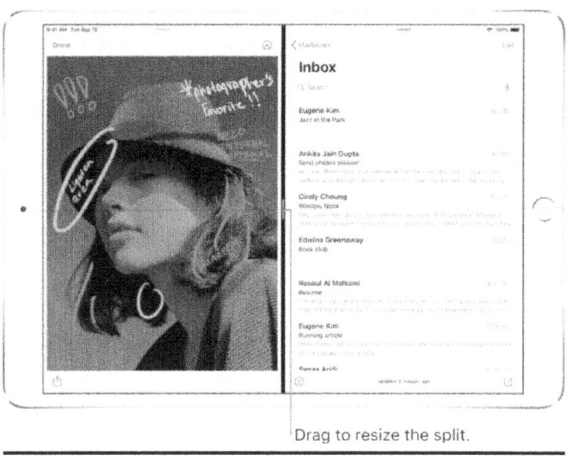

Drag to resize the split.

To close split view, you can:

Drag the app divider to the right or left edge of the screen, depending on the app that you wish to close.

You can turn Split View to Slide over by:

Swiping down from the top of the smaller view, and depending on the model of your device, you can simultaneously make use of Slide Over and Split View.

How to activate and deactivate multi-tasking feature

Ensure that the options for multiple apps and gestures are turned on in your iPad before you can use the multitasking feature.

To activate the multitasking feature, follow the instructions below:

1. Go to settings on your iPad.

2. Then navigate to Home Screen and Docks.

3. Then, Multitasking.

4. Then, turn on the switch that allows Multiple Apps, Gestures and Picture in Picture if they are not already enabled.

   To deactivate the multitasking feature on your Apple iPad, follow the steps below:

1. On your iPad, navigate to settings.

2. Touch General.

3. Next, click on Multitasking.

4. Touch "Allow Multiple Apps" to switch off the position.

5. Now, whenever you swipe from the right or left side of your iPad screen, the Split View or Slide Over multitasking will not be activated.

How to organize and manage files

Your Apple iPad is capable of organizing images, documents and other files into folders through the Files app.

How to create a Folder

You can create a folder by following the steps listed below:

1. Open an existing folder or a location on your Apple iPad device.

2. From the center of the screen, drag down and tap the New Folder button.

   Note: If you cannot find the New Folder button, you would not be able to create a folder in that location.

How to compress, rename and make any changes to a folder or file

Follow the instructions below, to make any changes to your folder or file I'm your iPad:

1. Press and hold down the folder or file, then choose any of the options: Compress, Rename, Copy, Duplicate, Delete or Move.

2. To modify multiple folders or files at the same time, touch Select, then touch your selections, and then touch your preferred option at the bottom of the screen.

   Note: Depending on the option you select, some options may not be available, for example you would not be able to move or delete an app library (a folder named with an app name).

How to tag a Folder or File

1. Press and hold down the folder or file, then touch Tags, then touch one or more tags.

2. Next, touch Done.

Note that items that you have tagged, will appear in the Browse Sidebar, below Tags.

To remove a tag, you can tap it again.

How to mark a Folder as Favorite

1. Press and hold down the folder, then touch Favorite.

2. Favorites usually appear in the Browser Sidebar.

How to view folder, and files in files on Apple iPad

From your Files app, you can open and view your images, documents and other files. To view files that have been recently opened, touch Recents which is located at the bottom of the screen.

To open and browse folders and files, follow the steps listed below:

1. Touch Browse located at the bottom of the screen and then touch an item in the Browse sidebar.

2. Touch Browse again, if you cannot see the Browse sidebar.

3. To open a folder, location or file, tap it.

   Note: If you have not installed the app that creates a file, you can find an opened preview of the file in Quick Look.

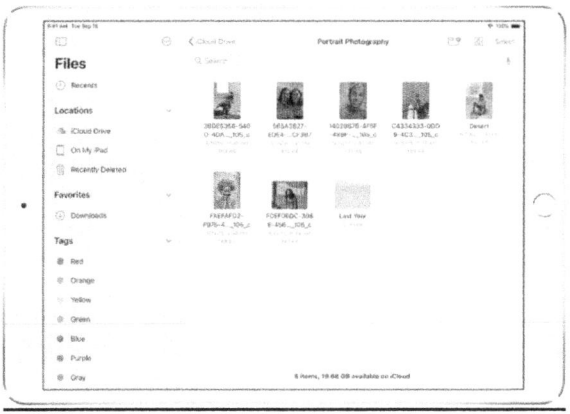

To change how folder and files are sorted:

1. Open any location, then drag down from the center of the screen and then touch Tags, Kind, Size, Date and name.

Rearrange the
sidebar.

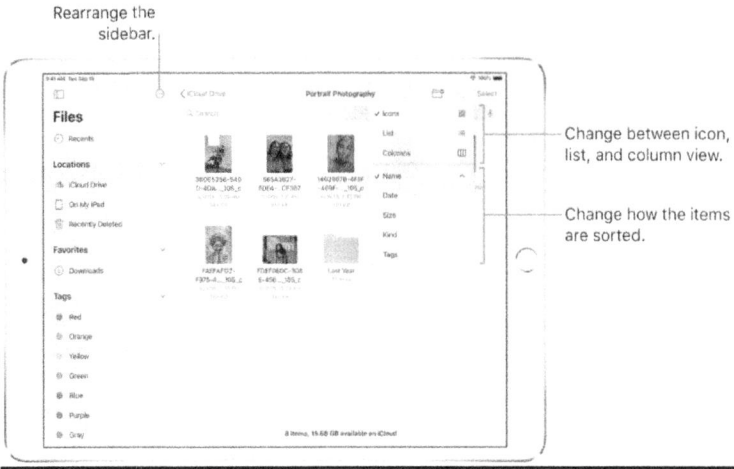

Change between icon,
list, and column view.

Change how the items
are sorted.

How to change to Column, List and Icon View

Locate an open folder or location, then drag down from the center of the screen and do any of the following:

1. View as Columns - Touch the Column view button.

2. View as Icons - Touch the List View button.

3. View as List - Touch the Grid View button.

You can look deeper into any folder hierarchy from the column view by tapping an item located in the right most column, and then by swiping left. You can see a preview of a file with its metadata (such as its size and kind) by tapping the file. (swipe left if you do not find the preview at the rightmost column.) Different actions and viewing of files can be performed without leaving Files.

Touch Open under the file preview in order to perform different actions and view the file without leaving Files.

How to find a specific folder or file

To do this:

1. First, in the search field enter a document type, folder name or file name.

2. When you then search, you have the option of:

○ Focusing the scope of your search: Below the field, touch the name of the tag or location or touch Recents.

○ Hiding the keyboard to see more results on your screen: To do this Touch the keyboard key.

○ Starting a new search: Touch the Clear Text button on the search field.

○ Opening a result: To open a result Touch it.

Rearranging the Browse Sidebar

To rearrange the side bar, Touch the More Button located at the top of the sidebar, then Touch Edit and then perform any of the following options:

1. Hiding a location, by turning off the location.

2. Delete and remove a tag from all items by Touching the Remove button located next to the tag.

3. Remove an item from the list of Favorites by Touching the Remove button located next to the item.

Making use of gestures on your iPad 8th Generation

Your Apple iPad 8th generation comes with simple and advanced gestures which can be used to interact with your iPad.

Simple Gestures

You can control your iPad and your apps by making use of simple gestures such as touch and hold, tap, zoom, scroll and swipe.

1. **Touch and Hold** : You can perform quick actions and preview contents by Touching and holding items in an app. To open a quick action menu, touch and hold an app icon briefly.

2. **Tap** : This gesture is used when one finger touches lightly on your iPad screen.

3. **Zoom** : Put two of your fingers on your screen close to each other. To zoom in, spread them apart and also zoom out by moving them towards

each other. A photo or a web page can also be double tapped to zoom in, and also zoomed out by double tapping again. On your Maps, you can zoom in by double tapping and holding the screen while dragging up, and dragging down to zoom out.

4. **Scroll** : To scroll, move one finger across the screen without lifting it. Take for example, in Photos, to see more you can drag a list down or up. You can also scroll quickly by swiping and then touching the screen to stop scrolling.

5. **Swipe** : To swipe, you move one of your fingers quickly, across the screen.

Advanced Gestures

You can control your Apple iPad and your apps by making use of advanced gestures to navigate to access controls, switch between recent apps, Home Screen and more. Some gestures are done differently with the Home button on your apple iPad:

1. **To go home**: You can return to your home screen by swiping up from the bottom edge of your screen at any time.

2. **Accessing controls quickly**: To access controls quickly, open the control center by swiping down from the top right corner, then press and hold the control to reveal more options. To remove or add controls navigate to settings, then Control Center.

3. **To open the App Switcher**: Swipe up from the bottom edge of your iPad, then pause in the center of your screen, and then release your

finger. Browse any open apps, swipe right and then touch the app that you wish to use.

4. **Switching between apps**: Swipe right or left along the bottom edge of your screen to switch quickly between open apps. If your Apple iPad has a Home button, swipe alongside a slight arc.

5. **Opening the Dock within an app**: From the bottom edge of your screen swipe up, then pause to reveal the Dock. Quickly open another app by tapping it in the Dock.

6. **To ask Siri**: Say "Hey, Siri" or touch and hold the top button and make your preferred request. If your iPad has a Home button, touch and hold the Home button then make your request. Siri usually listens until you let go of the button.

7. **Making use of the Accessibility Shortcut**: To do this triple click the top button. Or if your iPad has a Home button, you can triple click the Home button.

8. **Taking a Screenshot**: Press and quickly release the top button and the up volume button simultaneously. If your iPad has a Home button, press and release the top button and the Home button simultaneously.

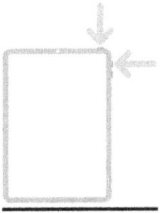

9. **To Turn off**: press and hold down the top button and any of the volume button simultaneously until the sliders appear, and then drag the slider at the top to power off. If your iPad has a Home button, touch and hold down the top button until the slider appears on your screen or navigate to settings, then General, then Shut Down.

10. **To force restart**: Touch and release the up volume button, and touch and release the down volume button, then you touch and hold the top button until you see the Apple logo on your screen.

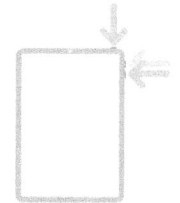

How to start up your iPad

To start up your device, follow the instructions listed below,

Turn on your device:

1. Press and hold the wake/sleep button until the Apple logo appears.

Top button

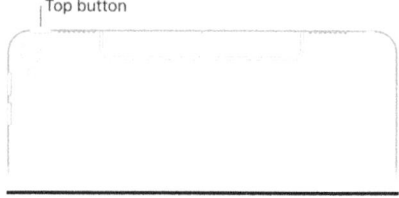

2. You will see "Hello written in different languages, press the home button to start.

CHAPTER TWO

How to restore Previous Data

You can return your Apple iPad settings to their default settings without erasing your contents. Ensure that your iPad is backed up before returning your iPad to their default settings, if you want to save your settings. For example, if you try to solve a problem, but returning your settings to default does not help in resolving the problem, you can try restoring your previous settings from a backup.

To do this:

1. Navigate to Settings, General and then Reset.

2. Next, choose any of the option below:

Note: All your contents on your Apple iPad will be removed, if you choose the option Erase All Content and Setting.

- **Resetting All Settings**: All settings which include, privacy settings, network settings, location settings, Apple Pay cards, and the Home Screen layout will be reset to its default or removed. None of your media or data will be deleted.

- **Resetting Network Settings**: All your network settings will be removed. In addition to this, the name given to devices in Settings, then General, then About will be reset to "iPad", and then manually trusted certificates for things such as websites will be changed to untrusted. Choosing this also turns off cellular data roaming.

When you reset your network settings, VPN and previously used settings which were not installed by mobile device management (MDM) or configuration profile will be removed. Your Wi-Fi will be turned off and then turned back on, thereby disconnecting you from any network which you are connected to. The Ask to Join Networks and Wi-Fi will remain turned on.

You can also remove VPN settings which were installed through a configuration profile by navigating to Settings, then General, then Profile and Device Management and then select the configuration profile, and then touch Remove Profile.

You can also remove settings installed by MDM, by navigating to Settings, then General, then Profiles and Device Management and then touch Management, then touch Remove Management. Doing this removes certificates and other settings that are provided by MDM.

- **Resetting Keyboard Dictionary**: Words can be added to your keyboard dictionary by registering letting suggested words by your iPad while typing. When you reset your keyboard dictionary, only words that you have added will be erased.

- **Resetting Home Screen Layout**: When you choose this option, it returns your iPad built in apps to the original layout on the Home Screen that came with the iPad.

- **Resetting Location and Privacy**: This option resets the privacy settings and location services to their default state.

Knowing about the new iPadOS 14

The new iPadOS 14 presents new compact designs for FaceTime and incoming phone calls. Siri and search interactions also helps users instaying focused on their tasks at hand. Apps on the new iPadOS 14 now have a new toolbar and sidebar that consolidates control in one place, which makes them more powerful and streamlined than ever before.

There is also a New Apple Pencil feature that includes Scribble for iPad, which delivers a new innovative way to work with handwritten notes, and AR Kit 4 that delivers a brand new Depth API which allows developers to create apps with more powerful features.

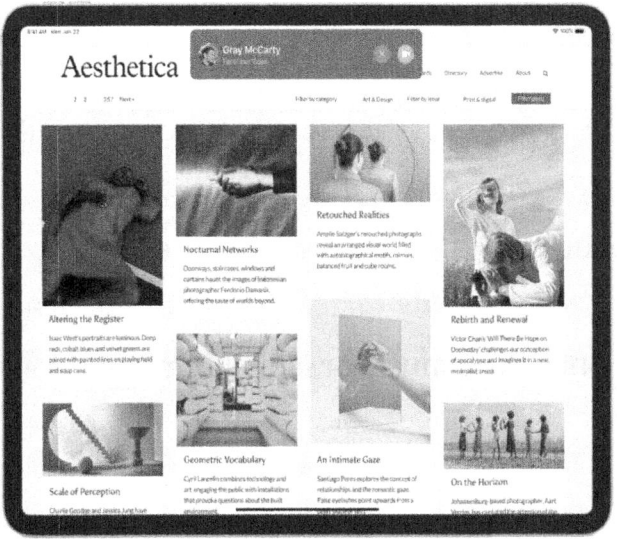

FaceTime and incoming phone calls

The new iPadOS 14 also presents all new compact designs for incoming phone calls and FaceTime, Search and Siri interactions which are particularly useful for your iPad and helps you in staying focused and being able to get more done in the moment. incoming phone calls and FaceTime are now presented in a lightweight banner, so that they do not take up your entire screen, therefore making it easier to quickly touch to answer the call or flick to dismiss so you get right back to your work. When activated, Siri is now presented at the bottom of the screen, therefore allowing you to reference information on your screen without interruption while making any request, and it also quickly gets out of the way when you are controlling music or launching other apps.

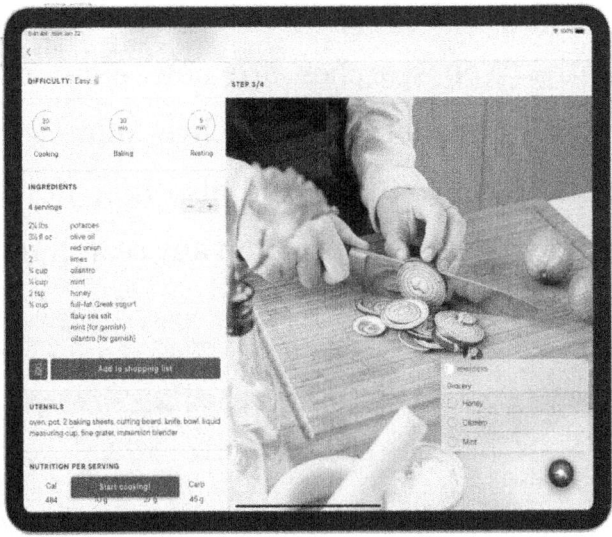

Search

The Search on the new iPadOS 14 has been rebuilt from scratch and is now capable as the one place of finding anything, ranging from launching and locating apps to

accessing files, contacts and getting quick information, to getting answers to questions which are common about places or people. With the new compact design, users can now start searching from anywhere on the iPad, without having the need to leave the app they are in currently. Web searches are now more refined and powerful, and they now deliver more relevant suggestions as you type and also they now have the ability to get with just a tap any search results.

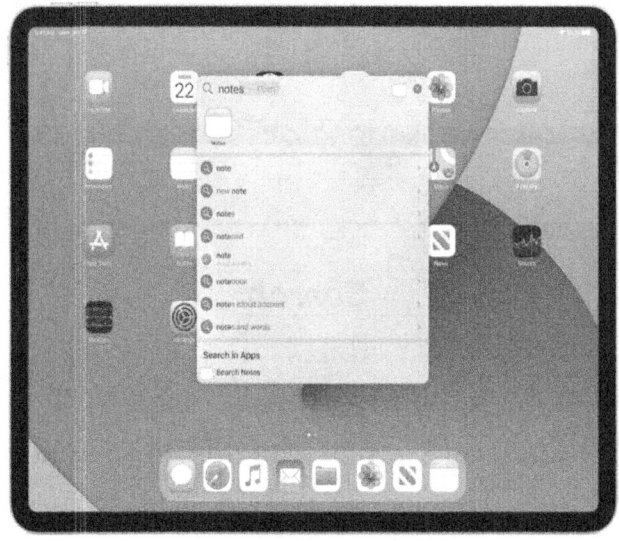

Sidebars

The Sidebars are now redesigned across many apps which includes Apple Music, Calendar,

Notes, Files, and Photos, which consolidates navigation into a single place, therefore making it now easier to navigate within any app while keeping your content front and center.

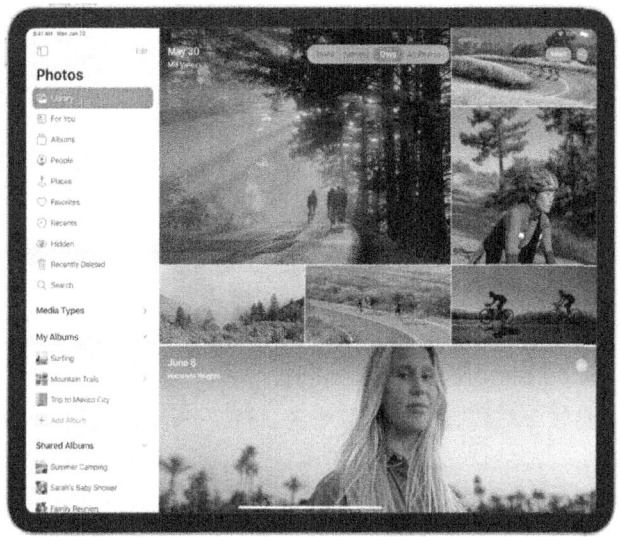

Toolbars

Also, the toolbars are streamlined with new pull down menus which provide access to app control in one place.

Hand written Notes and Apple Pencil

iPadOS 14 introduces Scribble to iPad with its new Apple Pencil, which allows you to write whatever you want in any text field (where it will be automatically covered to typed text) therefore making actions such as searching on Safari and replying to an iMessage easy and fast. All handwritten notes and conversion to text happens on the device, therefore keeping it secure and private.

When you take notes, Smart Selection makes use of on-device machine learning to differentiate between handwriting and drawings, therefore hand written text can be easily cut, pasted, and selected into another document as a type text. There is also an inclusive Shape right cognition that allows you to draw shapes which are made geometrically perfect and fit into the right place when adding useful illustrations and diagrams in Notes.

Also hand written text is now able to work with Data detectors to recognize dates, addresses and phone numbers in order to take actions like adding an event directly to your Calendar, tapping a written number in order to make a call and showing a location in Maps.

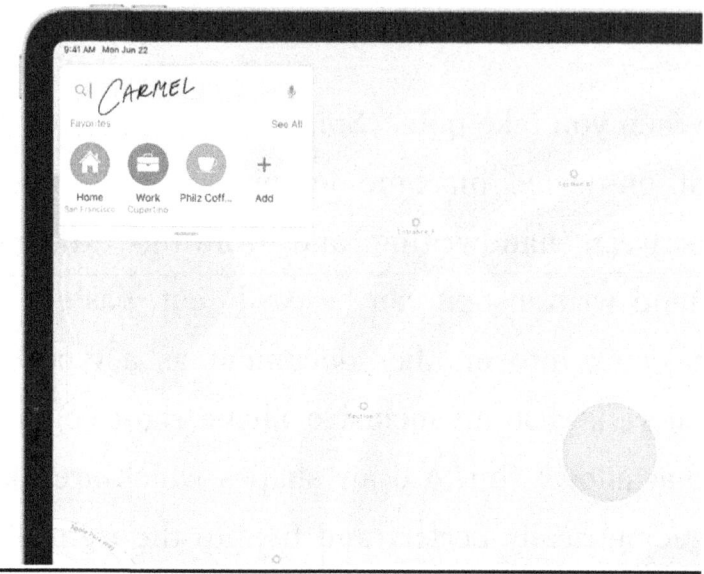

You can now write Chinese and English words together without the need to switch languages as Scribble offers support initially for Simplified and Traditional Chinese, English, and mixed Chinese and English.

Augmented Reality

Over time, augmented reality has proven to be a powerful technology which helps in accomplishing task ways never before thought possible. AR Kit 4 presents a brand new Depth

API which gives developers access to more precise depth information which are captured by the new LiDAR Scanner on Apple iPad Pro. Developers now can now make use of Depth API in order to drive powerful new features in their apps, such as testing how different paints will look before painting a room or taking body measurements for more accurate virtual try-on. AR Kit 4 introduces also Location Anchors for iPadOS apps and iOS, which leverages higher resolution data of the new map in Apple Maps, if available, to pin augmented reality experiences to any specific point in the world.

Enhanced Privacy Features

With iPadOS 14, all apps are now required to before tracking obtain the user's permission. As an addition, users are now able to upgrade their existing accounts Sign in with Apple, have the voice of choosing to share their approximate location with app developers rather than sharing their precise location when granting an app location permission or access, and even get more transparency into any app's usage of the camera and microphone.

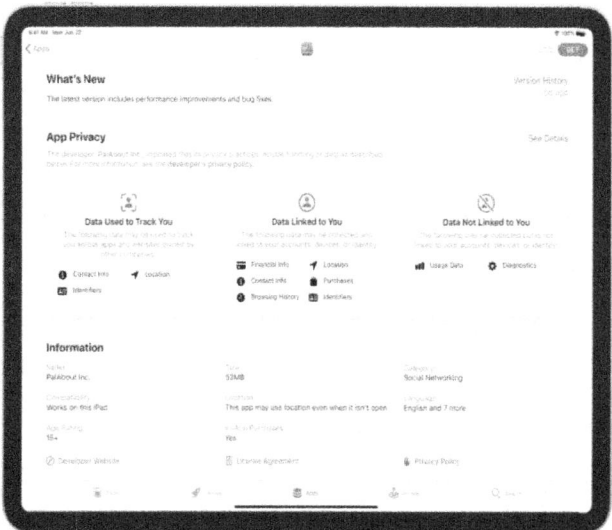

RAM and Storage of the iPad

The Apple iPad is packed with 3 GB RAM (Memory) while its internal storage is 32 GB and 128 GB.

How good the battery life is

The specification for the Apple iPad 8th Gen battery and power is as follows:

1. The battery is a built in 32.4-watt-hour rechargeable lithium-polymer battery.

2. Is capable of up to 9 - 10 hours of watching videos or surfing the web on Wi-Fi.

3. Capable of charging through USB to computer system or by power adapter.

4. Also capable of up to 9 - 10 hours of surfing the web by making use of cellular data networks.

5. The Apple iPad is also fueled with a Li-Po, (32.4 Wh) non-removable battery and the talk time ranges between 9 to 10 hours for multimedia.

Battery Life/Tips to Maximize Battery Life

To maximize your battery life, do the following:

1. Charge your iPad device properly for the first time after buying.

2. Use only a specified charger adapter.

3. Use only a specified USB cable.

4. Do Not use the device while charging.

5. Alternative power sources should not be the main method of charging.

Some features of the iPad 8th Generation

iPadOS14 features include the following:

1. An all new beautifully redesigned widget that shows timely information at a glimpse, and you can select from a Smart Stack of widgets, that makes use of on-device intelligence to surface the right widget based on factors such as activity, location and time.

2. Messaging is an important aspect to communicating with family and friends, therefore it is now easier to quickly access important

messages and stay connected. Conversations can now be pinned to the top your messages list so that you can keep up with lively group threads through inline replies or mention, and you can also now be able to customize further conversations, by creating a group photo making use of an emoji or image.

Also included on iPadOS 14 is the New Emoji option in Messages which comes more diverse and inclusive, with additional face coverings, hairstyles, head wear and more.

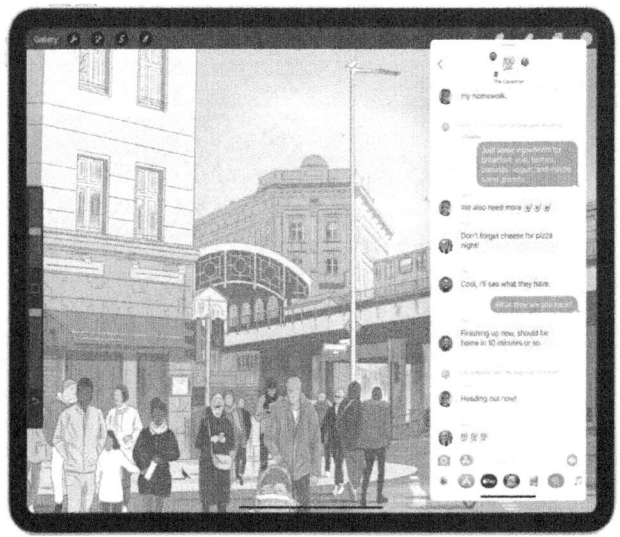

3. Siri now has expanded knowledge, which makes it capable of finding answers across the internet and is also capable of sending audio messages. When dictating email, notes, messages and more, the keyboard dictation runs on your device.

4. Maps now make it easier to explore and navigate with curated Guides and new cycling directions. Cycling directions now take into account how busy a street is, elevation and if there are stairs along the way. Guides now provide a curated list showing interesting places to visit in a city which are created by selected trusted resources that makes them a great way to find popular attractions, discover new restaurants and also explore new recommendations from respected

brands such as The Washington Post, Time Out Group, The Infatuation, Complex and All Trails, among others.

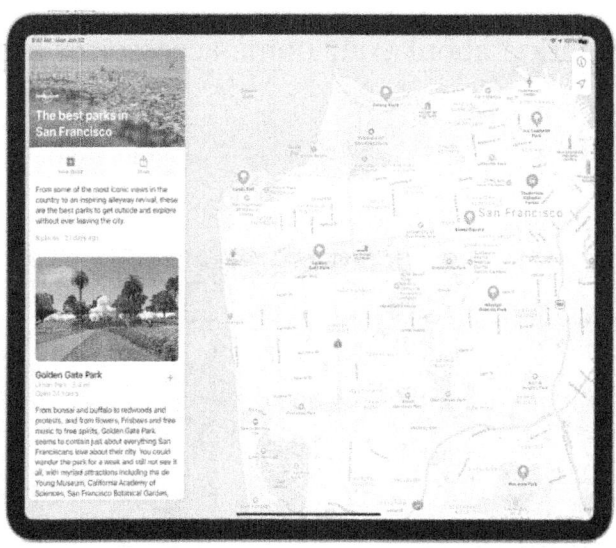

5. The Home app now comes with new automated suggestions and expanded controls in the Control Centre that makes smart home control easier by giving quicker access to scenes and accessories. Home Kit enabled light is now compatible with Adaptive Lighting to automatically adjust the

color temperature throughout the day and also on device Face Recognition which is compatible with cameras and video doorbells to identify family and friends. The Home Kit and Home app are built to be secure and private, therefore all information about your home accessories are end to end encrypted.

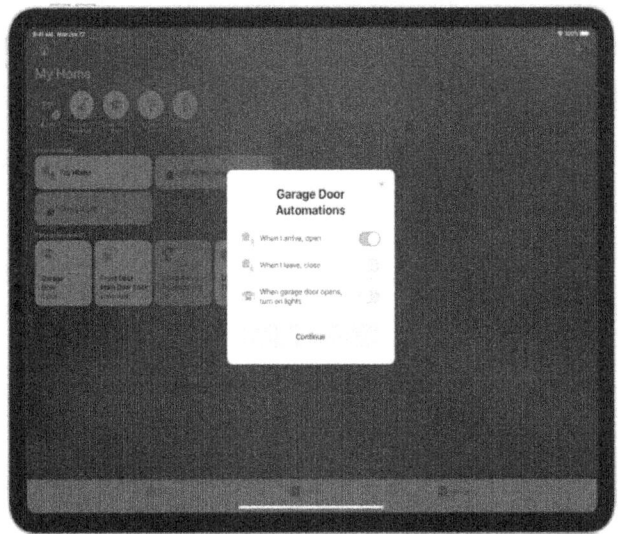

6. Safari offers a Privacy Report so that you can see easily which site trackers have been blocked by

your browser, and also it has secure password monitoring that helps you to detect passwords which have been saved on your browser and may have been involved in a data breach and also built in translation of an entire webpage.

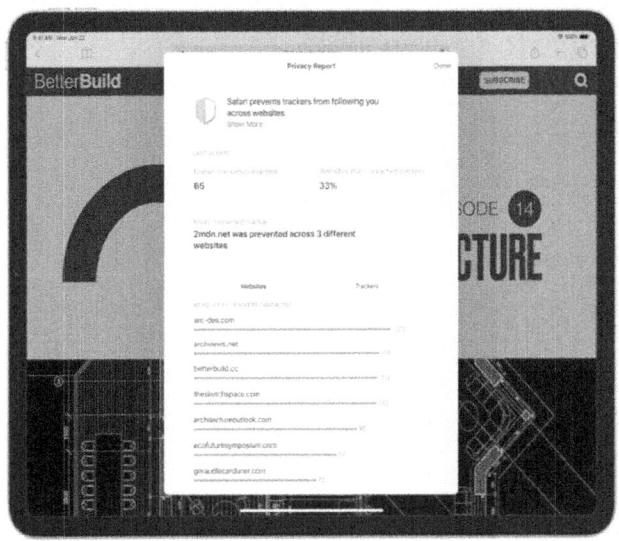

7. New accessibility features on iPadOS 14 includes Headphone Accommodations, that tunes and amplifies audio to help movies, phone calls, podcasts, and music sound clearer and crisper,

and also detection of sign language in Group FaceTime, that makes signing more prominent by a person in a video call. Also, the industry's leading screen reader for the blind community VoiceOver, is now capable of recognizing automatically what is displayed visually on screen, therefore more webs experiences are accessible to more people.

CHAPTER THREE

Understanding the Apple Smart keyboard

The apple Smart keyboard is a detachable, wireless accessory for your iPad that allows you to input text without the need to use the touch screen interface.

The apple Smart keyboard is 4 me thick and it comes with the standard 64 qwerty keys of commands, characters and letters. The keyboard connected your iPad tablet with the Smart Connector, which is a sensor placed alongside the edge of both devices that can also serve as the charger.

You can also attach this keyboard to your iPad in order to interact with it more like your Personal Computer or you can remove the keyboard and interact with the iPad tablet through its touch screen. When you attach the keyboard to your iPad, you will be able to fold the keyboard onto the screen to serve as a cover.

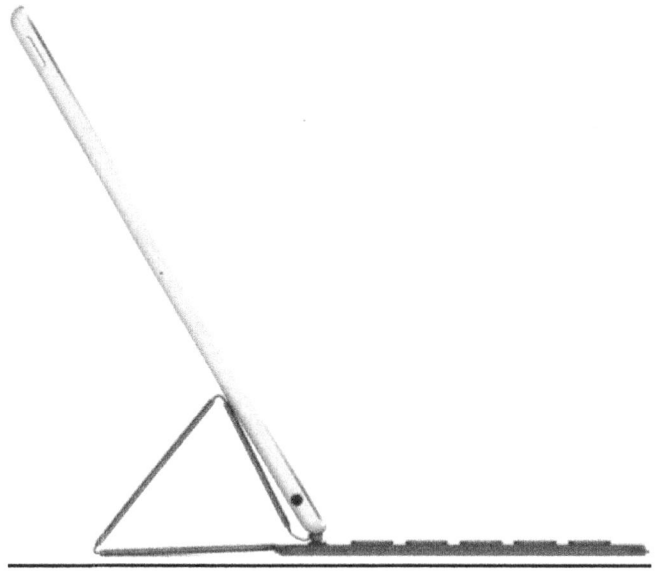

There are three layers which make up the Apple Smart keyboard, they include a microfiber lining for the screen protection, a polyurethane on top, and a conductive fabric in the middle which enables communication between the keyboard and tablet and enables charging of the battery. The keyboard finishes with a stain proof and water resistant coating.

The Apple Smart Keyboard integrates with iOS 14 to support keyboard shortcuts which perform quick actions such as switching between apps.

The Cameras of the iPad 8th Generation

The camera is an important app in the iPad 8th Gen device. In this section, you'll find a useful guide on how to make use of it.

The Apple iPad 8th Generation comes with the front (Selfie) and main back cameras. The iPad's selfie camera comes with a 1.2-megapixel sensor for photos and supports 720p for videos.

The main camera comes in an 8-megapixel camera for photos.

Take Amazing Photos

1. Open the camera app in photo mode and tap the shutter button to capture a photo.

Edit Your Photos

To edit photos, make use of the tools in the photo app to make edit to photos on your iPad device. If you make use of iCloud photos, any edit you make will be saved on all your Apple devices.

Adjust light and color

1. Capture a photo.

2. Tap the Edit button and select an effect like exposure, then use the slider to adjust it.

3. To see the shot before and after the effect was applied, tap the effect button.

4. Tap Done to save and finish up.

5. Tap discard to remove changes if you don't like it.

Using the Ultra Wide Camera

The ultra-wide camera feature on the iPad 8th Gen device allows users to capture a better field of view without needing an external lens. To use the feature, open the Camera app and tap the "0.5" to capture photos in ultra-wide view

Features of the cameras

The Apple iPad 8th Generation camera has the following features included in it:

1. 8-megapixel camera.

2. $f/2.4$ aperture.

3. Five element camera lens.

4. Features camera Hybrid IR filter.

5. Features camera Backside illuminations.

6. It features Live Photos.

7. It features Autofocus.

8. Features panorama which is up to 43MP.

9. Features HDR for photos.

10. Features Exposure control.

11. Features burst mode.

12. Features cameras Tap to focus.

13. Features camera Timer mode.

14. Features image Auto stabilization.

15. Body and face detection.

16. Features photo geotagging.

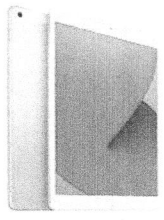

How to use video Recording

To use the video recorder on your iPad 8th generation, follow the instructions listed below:

1. Select your preferred Video mode.

2. Next, touch the Record button or you can press any of the volume buttons to start recording.

3. Zoom in or out of the video by pinching the screen.

4. Touch the Record button or you can press any of the volume buttons to stop the recording process.

Your Apple iPad by default records videos at 30 frames per seconds (fps). You can choose other types of frames depending on your model and video resolution settings by navigating to Settings, then Camera, then Record Video. Faster frame rates and higher resolutions leads to larger video files.

Note: A green dot will appear on the top of the screen when your camera is in use for your security.

Using quick toggles to change video frame rate and video resolutions

When you are in video mode, you can display quick toggles to change the frame rate and video resolutions that are available on your Apple iPad.

You can display quick toggles in video mode, by navigating to Settings, then Camera, then Record Video and then turn on the Video Format Control.

Recording slow motion videos

Follow the steps below to record a video in slow motion:

1. First, select Slo-mo mode.

2. Touch the Record button or you can press any of the volume buttons to stop or start recording.

   You can set a portion of the video to play in slow motion while the rest will play at regular speed by tapping the video thumbnail, then touch Edit. Define the section you wish to playback in slow motion by sliding the vertical bars located below the frame viewer.

   You can change the resolution and frame rate depending on your model. The higher your resolution and the faster your frame rate, the larger the resulting video file will be.

   Change Slo-mo recording settings by navigating to Settings, then Camera, then Record Slo-mo.

How to capture time lapse videos

To capture Time lapse video, follow the steps below:

1. Choose your preferred Time lapse mode.

2. Ensure that you set up your Apple iPad where you want to capture a moment, flowing traffic or any other experience over a period of time.

3. Start recording by tapping the Record button and tapping again to stop recording.

Adjusting Auto FPS settings

Apple iPad improves the video quality in low light situations by reducing automatically the frame rate to 24 fps, if your model supports Auto FPS.

To do this, navigate to Settings, then Camera, then Record Video, and do any of the following:

1. On iPad Air 4th generation, touch Auto FPS, then apply it to only 30-fps video or to both 30 and 60 fps video (iPadOS 14.2 or above).

2. On iPad Pro 11-inch and 12.9-inch 3rd generation and later, turn on Auto Low Light FPS.

Knowing more about the FaceTime HD camera

FaceTime; who can use it

The FaceTime app is a video calling app developed by Apple Inc. and can only be used on Apple devices such as iPads, iPhones, and MacBook.

Make/end a FaceTime call

1. Open the FaceTime app and tap the "+" button at the top of the screen.

2. Enter the name or number of the person you wish to call in the entry field.

3. Tap the video icon to make a video call or the audio icon to make an audio FaceTime call. (Available in select regions).

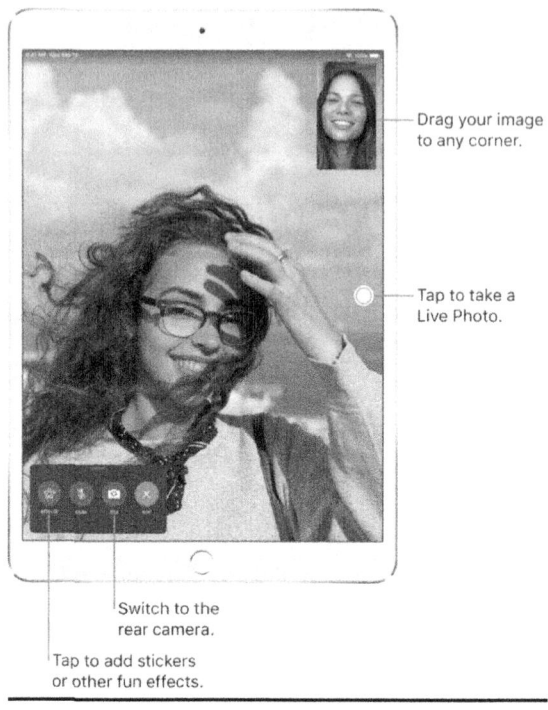

Drag your image
to any corner.

Tap to take a
Live Photo.

Switch to the
rear camera.

Tap to add stickers
or other fun effects.

Switch views

To switch views while on a FaceTime call, tap the selfie camera option to switch to your rear camera.

Set up iMessage

1. Open Settings and tap messages. (Enter that you have iMessage turned on).

2. Tap send and receive on the message page.

3. Tap "Use your Apple ID for iMessage" when it appears and sign in with your Apple ID.

4. Tap Done to finish setup.

Send Emoji's in place of texts

To send an Emoji in place of a text:

1. While on the message app, tap on the emoji button.

2. Select and tap your desired emoji.

3. To send the emoji, tap send.

How to leave a Message

If your Face FaceTime call is not answered by anybody, do any one of the following:

1. Touch to leave a message.

2. Touch Cancel to cancel the call.

3. Touch Call Back to try calling back.

How to start FaceTime from a message conversation

Form a message conversation, you can start a FaceTime call to the person with whom you are chatting with.

1. Touch the profile picture in the Messages conversation, then My Account button, or you can touch the name located at the top of the conversation.

2. Touch Call again.

To Call Again

To call again navigate to your call history, then touch the number or name, or you can touch the Info button in order to choose a number or name in Contacts.

How to receive a FaceTime Call

When a FaceTime call comes in on your Apple iPad, you can touch any of the following:

1. Accept: To take the call.

2. Decline: To decline the call.

3. Remind Me: To set a reminder so you can call back.

4. Message: To send a text message to the caller.

Send the caller
a text message.

Set up a reminder
to return a call.

If, when a FaceTime call comes in and you are on a regular call, instead of choosing Accept, you will see the End and Accept option, which will terminate your previous call and connect you to the incoming call.

Deleting a call from your call history

Swipe left over your call in your call history in FaceTime, and then touch Delete.

CHAPTER FOUR

How to beautify your Display

Display and Brightness

To access the Display and brightness settings, follow the steps below:

1. Open Settings, and click on accessibility.

2. On the screen that appears next, tap Display and Text size. (Now you are in the Display menu.)

To access brightness:

1. Following the steps above, turn on the Auto brightness feature or adjust it manually.

Adjusting your screen brightness manually

To make your apple iPad screen brighter or dimmer, make sure you do one of the following:

1. First open the Control Center, and then drag the Brightness button.

2. Go to Settings, then Display and Brightness, and then drag the Slider.

Adjusting your screen brightness automatically

In your Apple iPad, you can adjust the brightness of the screen for current light conditions by making use of the built in ambient light sensor.

To do this:

1. Navigate to Settings and then Accessibility.

2. Touch Display and Text Size, and then turn on the Auto Brightness.

Turning on or off the True Tone

True Tone can be turned on to automatically adapt the intensity and color of the display to match the light in your environment.

Turn on or off True Tone, by doing any of the following:

1. Open the Control Center, then tap and hold the brightness button, then touch the True Tone button to turn the True Tone on or off.

2. Navigate to Settings, then Display and Brightness, and then turn True Tone on or off

Set brightness and Night shift

Brightness and night shift can be set from the control center. To set brightness:

1. Open Settings, and tap display and brightness.

2. Use the slider to increase (right) or decrease (left) the brightness level.

To set night shift, refer to the next two subsections of this section.

About Night Shift

Night Shift makes use of the clock and geo-location of your device to know when it's night time, then it automatically adjusts your display color to a warmer one.

Ways to turn Night Shift on and off:

Below are some of the ways to turn on and off night shift:

1. In the control center, press the brightness control icon firmly, tap the icon to turn it off, and on.

2. Open Settings, tap Display, tap Night Shift.

Scheduling Night Shift to automatically turn on and off

You can make use of Night Shift to move the colors in your display to the warmer end of the spectrum at night and also to make viewing your screen easier on your eyes.

To do this:

1. Navigate to Settings, then Display and Brightness, and then Night Shift.

2. Then turn on Scheduled.

3. Drag the slider below Color Temperature towards the cooler or warmer end of the spectrum to adjust the color balance for Night Shift.

4. Touch From, then select either Sunset to Sunrise or choose Custom Schedule.

5. If you select Custom Schedule, touch the options to schedule the times that you want Night Shift to turn on and off.

6. If you choose Sunset to Sunrise, your Apple iPad makes use of the data collected from your clock and geolocation to determine when it is night time for you.

   Note: If your Location is turned off in Settings, then Privacy, the Sunset to Sunrise option will not be available, or if you turn off Setting Time Zone in Settings, then Privacy, Location Services, then System Services.

How to change the wallpaper on your iPad

On your Apple iPad, select a photo or an image as your wallpaper for the Home Screen or Lock Screen. You can make the choice from Still or Dynamic images.

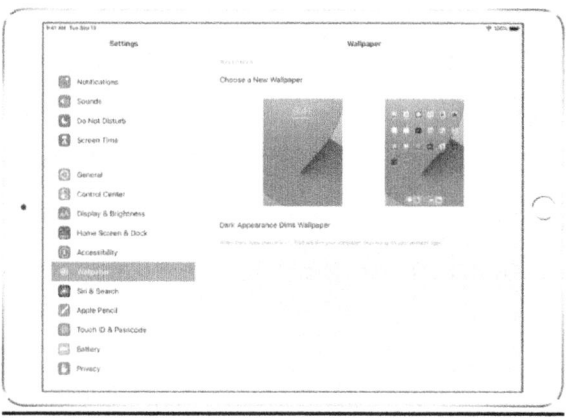

To change your wallpaper on your Apple iPad, follow the instructions below:

1. Navigate to Settings, then Wallpaper and Choose a New Wallpaper.

2. Then, do any of the following steps:

o Select a preset image from a group at the top of the screen such as Stills, Dynamic and so on.

o When Dark Mode is turned on, wallpapers that are married with the Appearance button changes appearance.

o Choose one of your own photos by tapping any album, then touching the photo.

o Reposition your selected image by pinching to zoom in on it, then drag the selected image to move it. To zoom back out, pinch closed.

o To turn on Perspective Zoom, touch the Parallax Effect button (only available with some wallpaper choices), that makes your wallpaper seem to "move" when your viewing angle is changed.

   Note: The option of Perspective Zoom does not appear if Reduce Motion which is located in Accessibility Settings is turned on.

3. Touch Set and then select any of the following:

- Set Lock Screen.

- Set Home Screen.

- Set Both.

You can turn on Perspective Zoom for wallpaper that you have already set, by navigating to Settings, Wallpaper, and then touching the image of the Home Screen or Lock screen, then touch Perspective Zoom.

Tip: Wallpaper can be set to automatically change by creating a personal automation in the Shortcuts app. Do this by setting a schedule for your automation, then adding the Set Wallpaper action to your automation.

How to use the Dark mode feature

The Dark Mode gives your entire iPad experience a dark color scheme that is perfect for use in low light environments. Dark mode can be set to turn on automatically at night or you can turn it on from the Control Center or you can use a custom schedule in Settings. With your Dark Mode turned on, you can make use of your Apple iPad while for example, reading on your bed, without disturbing the person right next to you.

To turn on Dark mode, do any of the following:

1. Open the Control Center, then touch and hold down the Brightness button, and then touch the Appearance button to turn Dark Mode on or off.

2. Navigate to Settings, then Display and Brightness, and then select Dark to turn on Dark Mode or choose Light to turn off Dark Mode.

Scheduling Dark Mode to automatically turn on and off

To do this:

1. Navigate to Settings, the Display and Brightness.

2. Then, turn on Automatic, and then touch Options.

3. Select either Custom Schedule or Sunset to Sunrise.

4. If you select Custom Schedule, touch the option to schedule the time that you want Dark Mode to turn on or off.

5. If you make the choice of Sunset to Sunrise, your Apple iPad will make use of the data collected from your geolocation and clock in order to determine when it is night time for you.

How to use the speak screen feature

If your VoiceOver is turned off, you can have your Apple iPad speak the entire screen or selected text. Apple iPad can also speak text corrections and provide feedback and suggestions as you type.

To change the speech settings on your Apple iPad:

1. Navigate to Settings then Accessibility, then Spoken Content.

2. Then adjust any of the following:

- **Speak Selection** - Touch the Speak button to listen to the text you selected.

- **Speak Screen** - Swipe down with two of your fingers from the top of the screen to listen to the white screen.

- **Speech Controller** - This shows the controller for easy and quick access to Speak on Touch and Speak Screen.

- **Highlight Content** - Apple iPad can highlight sentences, words, or both as they are spoken. You have the option of changing the highlight style or color.

- **Typing Feedback** - The typing feedback for external keyboards and on-screen can be configured and also you can choose to have the iPad speak entire words, each character, typing predictions, auto capitalizations, and auto corrections.

To listen to typing predictions, you need to go to Settings, then General, then Keyboards and then turn on Predictive.

- **Voices** - Select a dialect and voice.

- **Speaking Rate** - Drag the slider to do this.

- **Pronunciations** - Spell out or dictate how you want certain phrases to be spoken.

How to Hear your Apple iPad speak

Ask Siri something like; "Speak screen." or you can do any of the following:

1. **Hear selected text** - Choose the text, and then touch Speak.

2. **Hear the entire screen** - From the top of the screen, swipe down with two of your fingers. Make use of the controls that show to adjust the rate or to pause speaking.

3. **Hear typing feedback** - Start typing and then to hear typing predictions (if turned on) tap and hold each word.

CHAPTER FIVE

Knowing more about the Apple Arcade

Apple Arcade is a gaming service with a premium subscription that lets you download and play games that have a monthly fee. Apple announced that the Apple Arcade will be priced $4.99 per month including a one-month free trial which will be available to test it out. A single monthly subscription allows a maximum of six family members to access the games. To do this, you need to set up Family Sharing, which requires all family members to have the same credit card that is associated with their Apple ID.

Apple teamed up with big named gaming companies and indie developers to create "exclusive and new" games available for the Apple Arcade service. All content released through Apple Arcade are freshly created for Apple Arcade, therefore it does not include existing iOS games.

The game companies Apple worked with include: Konami, LEGO, Mistwalker Corporation, SEGA, Annapurna Interactive, Bossa Studios, ustwo games, Cartoon Network, Finji, Giant Squid, Klei Entertainment, Snowman, and other developers for Apple Arcade games. At the inception the arcade had over 50 games, but over time, Apple has steadily been adding new games on a regular basis, therefore there are now over a 100 games available to play on the Apple Arcade.

There is an Apple Arcade tab on your App Store in your iPad where you will find all of the games which are included in the Apple Arcade service. The editors of the Apple App Store have highlighted different titles, and made suggestions for you which will help you find new games to play.

How to insert SIMCARD on the iPad

To insert the Sim card on your Apple iPad, follow the instructions below:

1. First, locate the SIM tray.

2. The SIM tray is located at the lower right side of your iPad device. Insert the SIM, by inserting a SIM tool into the small hole to eject the SIM tray.

3. Insert or remove the SIM.

4. Insert the Nano-SIM into the SIM tray. makingsure that the gold contacts are faces down and the notched edge faces the upper right.

5. Next put the SIM tray into your iPad until it is put into place.

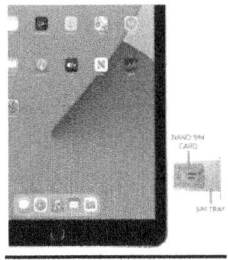

How to set and use the touch ID

Setting up Touch ID or Face ID

Touch ID:

1. From the settings app, touch the "Touch ID and Passcode" passcode.

2. Turn on any of the available options and follow the instructions that appear on your screen.

Face ID:

1. Open the settings app, and touch"Face ID and passcode", then touch set up Face ID.

2. To set up an extra appearance for your Face ID to recognize; open the Settings app, tap Face and Passcode, then set up an Alternate Appearance

and follow the instructions that appear on your screen.

CHAPTER SIX

How to backup with your Computer

Backup with iTunes On Pc or Mac

1. **Using** a specified USB cable, connect your iPad device to your PC.

2. Click the iPad button near the top left corner of the iTunes window on the iTunes App on your PC.

3. Click summary, then click backup.

4. To secure your backup, click the Encrypt Local Backup, then type a password, and click the "Set password" option.

Backup iPad using your Mac

1. Using a specified USB cable, connect your iPad device to your Mac.

2. Select iPad on the Finder sidebar on your Mac.

3. Click General at the top of the Finder window, then select "Backup all of the data on your iPad to this Mac."

4. Then click Backup Now.

Backup iPad using your Windows PC

1. Connect your window PC with your iPad using a USB cable.

2. On the window that pops up, select My computer.

3. Copy all necessary backup files from your iPad to your window PC.

4. When done, disconnect both devices.

More about Connectivity

In this section, you will find important information about connectivity.

Using A Mouse On Your iPad

On your iPad device, you can make use of a mouse instead of using your fingers. Using a mouse works just the same way it would on a MacBook.

Pair Magic Mouse or other Bluetooth mouse

1. Open Settings, then tap Bluetooth and turn it on.

2. Select the Magic Mouse device when it appears.

3. Type "0000" if you are asked for a pin, otherwise, tap Pair.

Connect to A Wi-Fi Network

1. Open Settings, Wi-Fi, then turn it on.

2. Tap on a Wi-Fi network you want to join. (You might be asked to provide a password).

Air pods/Share Music Through Air pods

1. Tap the Airplay icon in the app you are listening to, then tap Share Audio.

2. Hold both devices close with the Air Pods in the case and the lid opened (Air Pods&Air Pods pro.)

3. For Air Pods max, just hold it close to your device.

Pair Air Pods with your iPad

1. Open Settings and select Bluetooth, then turn it on.

2. On the Home Screen of your iPad do either of the following:

   ○ Air Pods or Air Pods pro: Open the case and hold it close to your device.

   ○ Air Pods max: hold it close to your device then press the noise control button on the right headphone.

3. Follow the instructions on your screen and tap Done.

Stop/Pause the audio

To stop or pause an audio from your lock screen, simply tap the "Pause" button.

Skip tracks

Tap the "Next" button to skip a track.

Using The Smart Keyboard

The Smart keyboard is a portable full size keyboard that connects to an iPad via Smart Connector.

All you need to do is attach the keyboard to your iPad and start typing.

More about Siri

Siri is the official artificial intelligence assistant for Apple devices. In this chapter, you'll find out how to properly use Siri. Let's begin!

Activating Siri

If you did not set up Siri when you first set up your iPad;

1. Go to Settings, then click Siri and Search.

2. Choose whether to turn on Siri with voice or button.

Summon Siri with a button

1. Activate the turn on Siri with button feature with the steps in the subsection above.

2. Press the top/home button to summon Siri.

What can Siri do

There are a lot things Siri can go such as;

1. Setting an alarm or reminder.

2. Search the web for you.

3. Dial a number.

4. Open an app.

5. Play music and more.

How to use the voice control feature

Your Apple iPad can be controlled with your voice. You canalso navigate voice commands with gestures and commands as you dictate or edit your text, and also see names or numbers next to screen elements.

To Set up Voice Control, follow the steps below:

1. Navigate to Settings, then Accessibility, then Voice Control.

2. Touch Set Up Voice Control.

3. You can then set any of the following options:

- **Language** - You can set the language and also download languages for offline use.

- **Customize Commands** - Create new commands and view available commands.

- **Vocabulary** - Teach new words to Voice Control.

- **Show Confirmation** - A visual confirmation will appear at the top of the screen when Voice Control recognizes a command.

- **Play Sound** - An audible sound is played when Voice Control recognizes a command.

- **Show Hints**: View hints and command suggestions.

- **Overlay**: Displays names, grid, or numbers, over screen elements.

- **Attention Aware**: Voice Control will wake you up when you look at your iPad and will go to sleep when you look away if your iPad comes with a Face ID.

Turning Voice Control on or off

After setting up Voice Control, it can be turned quickly on or off by making use of any of the following methods:

1. Summon Siri then say ``Turn off Voice Control" or "Turn on Voice Control."

2. Add Voice Control to Accessibility Shortcuts by navigating to Settings, then Accessibility, then Accessibility Shortcut, and then touch Voice Control.

Learning Voice Control commands.

You can say the following commands when the Voice Control is turned on:

1. "Open Control Center."

2. "Go Home."

3. "Tap item name."

4. "Open app name"

5. "Take Screenshot."

6. "Turn up volume."

Using the Screen Overlay

Navigate your Apple iPad with a screen overlay showing item names, grid or numbers for faster interactions.

1. **Item names**: You can say "Show names continuously," or "Show names" and then say "Tap item name."

2. **Numbers**: You can say "Show numbers" or say "Show numbers continuously," and then say the number next to the item you want.

3. **Grid**: Interact with a screen location that is not represented by an item number or name, say "Show grid continuously" or say "Show grid," and then say the number that is closest to the location you want. Zoom in on the location by saying another number on the smaller grid.

   Turn off the overlay by saying "Hide grid," or "Hide names," or "Hide numbers."

How to use the VoiceOverfeature

Setup & Use voice over:

1. Summon with and say "Turn on/off voiceover." Or open Settings, tap accessibility, then tap voiceover, then tap the toggle button to turn off or on.

CHAPTER SEVEN

Create Emoji

You can create anEmoji to match your mood and personality, and then send it in FaceTime or Messages. And if you have a compatible iPad, you can create an animated Emoji that makes use of your voice and also mirrors your facial expressions.

Creating your Emoji

1. Open your Messages app and then touch the Compose button to start a new message or navigate to an existing message.

2. Touch the Emoji button and then swipe right and touch the Add New Emoji.

3. After the above, you can then customize the features of your Emoji such as the eyes, nose, hairstyles, glasses, skin tone and more.

4. Finally, touch Done to finish.

Setup and use Map

Favorite in Apple Maps

In the maps app, you can save places you go often to in your favorite place such as your home, work, the coffee shop you visit often, and more.

Quickly find your favorites

1. To see favorites, swipe up from the top of the search card.

2. Swipe the row of favorites left or tap See All above the row to see more.

Edit a favorite

1. From the top of the search card, swipe up to show favorites, then tap the "See All" above the row of favorites options.

2. Tap the Edit icon next to the favorite.

   Based on the location, you might be able to perform the following changes:

1. Rename the favorite: tap the title of the place and rename.

2. Change the address: Tap the address and tap the open contact card.

3. Change the label.

4. Delete the location from your favorites list: Tap the location and remove Favorite.

5. Tell someone your ETA.

3. Done to finish up

Delete a place from your favorites

- From the top of the search card, swipe up to show your favorite.

- Tap the "See All" which is above the row of favorites.

- Swipe the item left.

Use 'look around feature' to navigate cities

1. When in a city, tap on the map apps or information card.

2. Do any of the following to change the view:

- Pan: drag your finger right or left.

- Move forward by tapping the scene.

- Pitch open or close to zoom in or out.

- View another interest point.

- Switch from or to full screen view.

- Hide labels in full screen view.

3. Tap Done when finished.

Transit Directions, Ride Sharing & Walking directions

1. To get transit direction, do any of the following:

- You can say something like "Hey Siri, give me transit directions to the Empire State Building." (this feature is not available in all countries.)

- Then tap your destination (landmark), then tap directions, bus transit icon.

- Touch and hold down any spot on the map then tap directions, bus transit icon.

2. Tap Leaving Soon to choose a transit date or time, then choose a time for departure/arrival.

3. Tap route card, then scroll down to the bottom and choose an option to select which transit vehicle you want.

4. On the route you want, tap Go.

Ride sharing

Ride sharing involves a use of an independent car company for a ride. Using the Apple maps, you can check routes before ordering a ride sharing service.

Walking directions

1. To get walking direction, do any of the following:

- Say something like "Hey Siri, give me walking directions to the coffee shop"

- Tap your landmark destination, then tap directions, then the walking icon.

- Touch down and hold any spot on the map, and tap directions, then the walking icon.

2. On the route you want, tap Go.

Setup Apple ID

Apple ID

An Apple ID is a means of authentication that is used by an iPad, Mac, iPhone, and other Apple devices. It contains the information about the person who created it and their device settings, and files. The Apple ID is used to log into your Apple device.

100

Sign in with your Apple ID

1. Open the settings app, and tap sign in to your iPad.

2. Type in your Apple ID and password. (If you don't have an apple ID yet, then you create one.)

3. If your Apple account was previously protected by a two-factor authentication, then enter the 6-digit code.

Transfer Money from Apple Cash to Your Visa Debit Card or Bank Account

You can from your Apple Cash card transfer money instantly or within one to three business days.

Transferring money to your Visa debit card or to your bank account

You can transfer money from your Apple Cash card by either making use of a bank transfer to send the money to your bank account within one to three days or you can make use of Instant transfer to send money to any eligible Visa debit card within 30 minutes. You can also make use of the Messages app to send money to an individual.

Making use of Instant Transfer

Ensure that your iPad has the latest version of iPadOS, then add an eligible Visa Debit card in the wallet app, and then make an instant transfer by:

1. Navigate to your card information, by opening the Settings app, then tapping Wallet and Apple Pay, then Touch your Apple Cash card.

2. Touch Transfer to Bank.

3. Input the amount and then touch Next.

4. Add a Visa debit card if you have not added one by tapping Add Card and then follow the instructions shown on your screen to add the Visa debit card.

5. Touch > to select the Visa credit card that you want to transfer funds to and choose the billing information for your chosen debit card.

   Funds are usually transferred within 30 minutes.

Transferring in one to three business days

1. Navigate to your card information, and open the Settings and, then touch Wallet and Apple Pay, then tap your Apple Cash card.

2. Touch Transfer to Bank.

3. Input the amount and touch Next.

4. Touch 1-3 Business Days, and if you do not have a bank account we up, follow the on screen instructions to add one.

5. Confirm with Touch ID, passcode or Face ID.

6. Then wait for the money to transfer, which usually takes 1 to 3 business days.

   Note: Children and teens less than 13 years old can transfer money from their Apple Cash account to a bank account and also transfer money to their bank account or any eligible Visa debit card by making use of Instant Transfer.

Updating your Bank Account Information

1. Navigate to your card info, and then open the Settings app, and then touch Wallet and Apple Pay, then touch your Apple Cash card.

2. Touch the Bank Account and then touch the bank account that you wish to update.

3. Delete your banking information by tapping Delete Bank Account Information. Then touch again to confirm. After deleting, different information or your bank information can be added.

4. Edit your bank information by tapping next to your account number or routing number, and then add your information, and then confirm the numbers and touch Next.

5. After updating your information on one apple device, it will automatically update on all your devices that Alton have signed in with your Apple ID.

Transfer Limits

Up to $10,000 per transfer and up to $20,000 within a seven-day period can be transferred from your Apple Cash to your Bank account. Money can only be transferred to any Bank in the United States and there are no fees attached to transferring your money from Apple Cash to your bank account, unless you make use of Instant Transfer.

Set Up Family Sharing On iPad

Family sharing requires you the organizer to first sign in with your Apple ID and confirm the Apple ID you use for everything including Apple Books, App Store and iTunes Store.

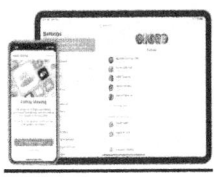

1. Navigate to Settings, then your name, then Family Sharing and then follow the instructions

displayed in your screen to set up your family group.

You can create an account for your child or add family members.

2. Touch the feature you wish to share, and then follow the instructions on your screen.

You can also learn more about Family sharing features by viewing the following on:

1. Subscriptions and iCloud storage.

2. Purchases.

3. Locations.

4. Features for children.

You may be asked to set up a subscription depending on the feature you chose. If you choose to share book purchases, TV, movie, music, and App Store with your family members, you therefore agree to pay for any purchases that they initiate while being part of the family group. Teen and adult family members can for themselves turn off purchase sharing.

Calendars, photos and more are also shared with family members.

CHAPTER EIGHT

How to Use the Magnifier Feature

Use magnifier

1. **Open** accessibility control, adjust zoom level (drag left or right) to turn on magnifier

2. Drag grabber up to show more control, adjust brightness, contrasts, and color filter.

Save a magnified object as an image

1. Drag the slider to adjust magnification, then tap the iPad screen to focus on the image, then touch and hold the image to save.

2. Tap save image to finish.

How to Use the Dictation Feature

On your Apple iPad, instead of typing you can use the dictation feature, but you have to ensure that

Enable Diction is turned on by navigating to Settings, then General, and then keyboard.

Note: Dictation is not available in all regions, countries and languages.

Turn on dictation by:

1. Navigating to Settings, then General, and then keyboard.

2. Then turn on Enable Dictation.

Dictating Texts

1. Touch the Dictate key on the on-screen keyboard, and then speak.

2. Ensure that Enable Dictation is turned on in Settings, then General, and then keyboard, if you do not see the Dictate key.

3. After you've finished, touch the Keyboard key.

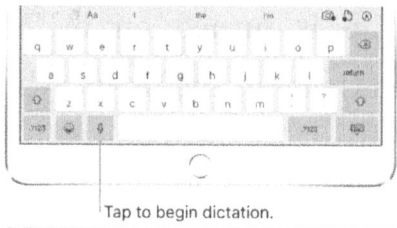

Tap to begin dictation.

To insert text by dictating, touch to place the insertion point, and then tap the Dictate key. The selected text can be replaced by dictating.

CHAPTER NINE

How to back up your iPad 8th Generation

Backup Using ICloud

1. **Open** the settings app, click on your name, then click iCloud Backup.

2. Turn on the iCloud backup. (When connected to power, locked, and on Wi-Fi, your iPad device will automatically back up daily.)

3. To manually backup, tap Back Up Now.

Turn On Ask to Buy

When Family sharing is set up, the family organizer can require that person's I'm the family group request approval for free downloads or purchases. Purchases can be approved by the organizer or guardian or parent in the family group.

Do this by:

1. Navigating to Settings, Your Name, then Family Sharing.

2. Touch Ask to Buy, and then do any of the following:

○ If you have no child in your family group, Touch Create a Child Account or touch Add Child.

○ If you have a child in your family group, touch the child's name and the. Turn on Ask to Buy.

Note: The age restriction for Ask to Buy varies by region. In the United States for example, the family organizer can turn on Ask to Buy for any member of the family under 18, while it is turned on by default for children under the age of 13.

Hide App Store Purchase

To hide App Store purchase:

1. Open the App Store app.

2. Touch the photo or the account button located at the top of the screen.

3. Touch purchased, of if you use Family Sharing, touch My Purchases.

4. Find the app that you have chosen, then swipe left on it and touch Hide.

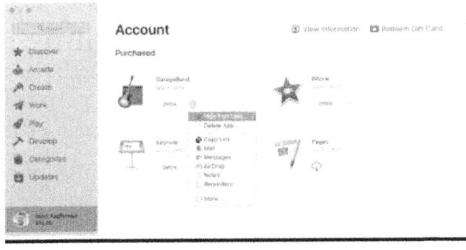

5. Next, touch Done.

CHAPTER TEN

Finding Lost Device ofa Family Member On The iPad

When family members who are in a Family Sharing group, share their location with you, you will be able to use the Find My app on your iPad to help another member in locating their lost device.

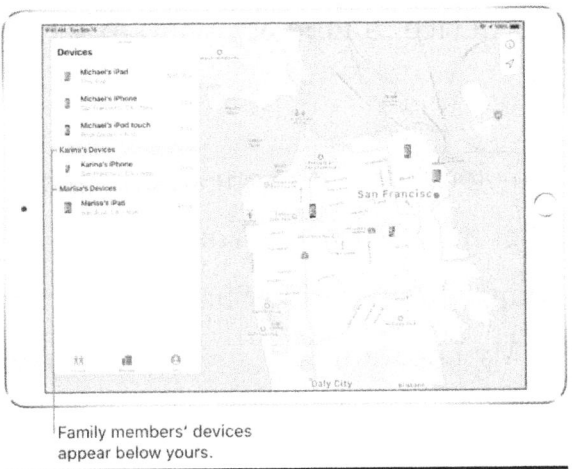

Family members' devices
appear below yours.

Setting up your iPad to be found by a family member

A family member can help locate your missing device if one of the following is done before the device is lost:

1. Ensure that Location Services are turned on by navigating to Settings, Privacy and then turn on Location services.

2. Ensure that Turn On Find my iPad is turned on by navigating to Settings, Your Name, Find My, Find My iPad, and then turn on Find My iPad, Find My network and then Send Last Location.

See Add a device to Find My iPad, to set up other devices.

3. Share your location with your family members by navigating to Settings, Your Name, Family Sharing and then Location Sharing, and then turn on Share My Location.

Share iCloud Calendar On iPad

From your calendar app, you are able to share an iCloud calendar with other iCloud users. When a calendar is shared by you, others will be able to see it, and you can let them change or add events. You can also share a read only version which anyone can view but would not be able to make changes to it.

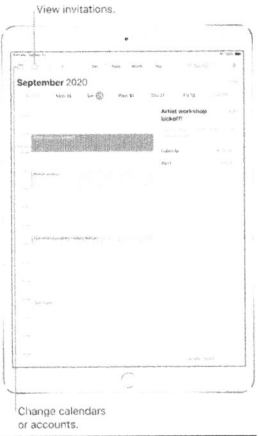

View invitations.

September 2020

Change calendars
or accounts.

Creating an iCloud Calendar

1. Touch the Calendar button.

2. Touch Add Calendar.

3. Type a chosen name for the new calendar and then touch done.

Sharing an iCloud Calendar

iCloud calendar can be shared with one or more people on iCloud, and those who you invite will receive an invitation to join the calendar.

1. Touch the Calendar button.

2. Touch the info button next to the iCloud calendar that you want to share.

3. Touch Add Person, then input an email address or a name, or you can touch the Add button to browse your contacts.

4. Touch Add.

Made in the USA
Monee, IL
05 June 2021